THE TRAUMA-INFORMED REVOLUTION

A Practical Guide to Healing and Recovery for Practitioners, Educators, and Policymakers in Building a Better Future For All.

Marley Kayswitch,

One

UNDERSTANDING TRAUMA: ITS NATURE AND IMPACTS

Trauma is an extremely upsetting event that surpasses a person's capacity for adjustment, leaving them feeling afraid, helpless, or powerless. It can significantly and permanently affect a person's psychological, emotional, and physical health.

What's a trauma?

Trauma is more than just an upsetting incident. It is a very subjective and individualized feeling that can be brought on by a variety of things, such as:

Emotional trauma: This includes abuse, neglect, and witnessing violence.

Physical trauma: This includes accidents, violence, and injuries.

Psychological trauma: This involves being exposed to situations that compromise or endanger one's sense of security or safety.

Sexual trauma: This includes sexual assault, abuse, and harassment.

Trauma's effects might differ substantially from person to person. But among the typical signs of trauma are:

Intrusive memories and thoughts:

Traumatised individuals may have intrusive memories, flashbacks, or nightmares related to the traumatic incident.

Avoidance behaviors: Traumatized individuals may steer clear of individuals, locations, or activities that evoke recollections of the traumatic incident.

Depressive and anxiety symptoms: Individuals who have experienced trauma may feel depressed, anxious, guilty, shamed, or find it difficult to focus.

Changes in behavioral and physical health:

Changes in sleep, hunger, energy levels, and physical health are possible among traumatized individuals. They might also partake in dangerous activities like drug misuse or self-harm.

Trauma can have a gravely detrimental effect on a person's life if it is not treated. It may result in:

Physical health problems: Trauma can also result in physical health issues like heart disease, chronic pain, and autoimmune disorders.

Mental health problems: Trauma is a major risk factor for the development of mental health issues like post-traumatic stress disorder (PTSD), depression, and anxiety.

Challenges in relationships:

Social problems: Trauma can make it challenging to establish and maintain healthy relationships. Social disengagement and retreat from interests and activities can result from trauma.

THE PRINCIPLES OF TRAUMA-INFORMED CARE

An approach to care known as trauma-informed care (TIC) acknowledges the pervasiveness of trauma and its effects on people as well as families. It seeks to provide trauma survivors with a secure, encouraging, and empowered atmosphere.

The following are the tenets of trauma-informed care:

1. **Safety**: Making sure that people's and families' emotional and physical safety is a primary concern.

2. **Transparency and trustworthiness:** Establishing transparency and trustworthiness with people and families via actions and communication that are truthful, upfront, and consistent.

3. **Peer support and mutual self-help:** Promoting among traumatized persons and their families peer support and mutual self-help.

4. **Collaboration and mutuality**: Developing individualized care plans and attending to the needs of individuals and families through cooperative efforts.

5.**Empowerment, voice, and choice:** Offering families and people the knowledge and ability to make decisions about their treatment and a voice in their own healing.

6. **Gender, historical, and cultural issues:** Understanding and honoring the ways in which gender, culture, and history can affect how people experience and deal with trauma.

Trauma-informed care implementation calls for a thorough strategy involving every facet of an organization or system, such as:

Culture of the organization: fostering a climate of support, safety, and trust across the board.

Staff training: Constantly educating staff members about the fundamentals of trauma-informed care and how to best assist traumatized individuals and their families.

Policies and procedures: Creating trauma-informed policies and processes that demonstrate the organization's dedication to empowerment, safety, and trust.

Service delivery: From the first point of contact to continuing treatment, integrating trauma-informed approaches into all facets of service delivery.

Community engagement: interacting with the community to encourage trauma-informed practices and increase understanding of trauma.

Organizations and institutions can provide a more healing and supportive environment for traumatized individuals and families by implementing a trauma-informed strategy. This may result in better results for people and families as well as lessen the general negative effects of trauma on society.

IDENTIFYING AND ASSESSING TRAUMA IN INDIVIDUALS AND COMMUNITIES

The first step in offering the right kind of care and support to people is recognizing and evaluating trauma in both individuals and communities. In order to properly intervene, one must be able to identify the signs and symptoms of trauma, which can have a deep and long-lasting effect on a person's life.

Determining a Person's Trauma

A person may exhibit several symptoms and indicators that point to their history of trauma. These fall into three general categories:

Intrusive memories and thoughts: Traumatized individuals may have intrusive memories, flashbacks, or nightmares related to the traumatic incident.

Avoidance behaviors: Traumatized individuals may steer clear of individuals, locations, or activities that evoke recollections of the traumatic incident.

Detrimental alterations in mood and cognition: Trauma survivors may struggle to focus or feel depressed, anxious, guilty, or ashamed.

Apart from the aforementioned broad indications and manifestations, there exist several distinct indications and symptoms that are linked to distinct categories of trauma. People who have encountered sexual trauma, on the other hand, might struggle with intimacy or have flashbacks of the assault. Those who have experienced physical trauma, on the other hand, might have physical injuries or chronic pain.

It is crucial to remember that not every victim of trauma will exhibit symptoms. While some people may experience symptoms that manifest long after the traumatic incident or that start slowly, others may be able to move past their experiences with no long-term effects.

Evaluating Trauma in Specific Persons

A multitude of instruments and techniques are available for evaluating trauma in humans. These can be roughly categorized into two groups:

Medical evaluation: A mental health expert will conduct a clinical interview to evaluate the person's symptoms, past experiences, and present functioning.

Normalized evaluations: These are self-report tools, such as questionnaires, that can be used to identify or screen for problems linked to trauma.

The particular instruments and techniques employed will change based on the needs of the person being assessed as well as the environment in which it is being carried out. All evaluations should, therefore, be carried out with consideration for the experiences of the individual and with sensitivity and cultural competence.

Determining Trauma in Societies

Communities can be significantly impacted by trauma as well. There are other ways to look at this, including:

High rates of violence: Residents in communities with high rates of violence may also be more likely to have experienced trauma.

Desirable mental health outcomes: Communities with high trauma rates may also have higher rates of mental health issues like anxiety, depression, and post-traumatic stress disorder (PTSD).

Social difficulties: Substance misuse, criminality, and school dropout are just a few of the social problems that can result from trauma.

It can be more challenging to recognize trauma in communities than in individuals. This is due to the fact that trauma frequently has a cascading effect that affects several generations and a community's general well-being.

Evaluating Stress in Societies

To evaluate trauma in communities, a variety of techniques can be applied. These consist of:

Focus groups: These can be used to collect qualitative information on the experiences of community members who have been impacted by trauma.

Community surveys: These can be used to collect data on the prevalence of trauma-related symptoms and experiences in a community.

Mapping the community: This can be used to pinpoint communities' areas that could be more traumatized than others.

Upon identification of trauma within a community, it is imperative to devise a comprehensive plan to address the issue. This could involve:

Promoting community resilience: This entails assisting a community in acquiring the knowledge and tools necessary to deal with trauma and foster healing.

Providing trauma-informed care: This entails providing care that is sensitive to the needs of individuals and families who have experienced trauma.

Advocating for policy change: This entails making an effort to alter laws and customs that exacerbate trauma in local communities.

Through the identification and evaluation of trauma in both individuals and communities, action can be taken to mitigate and prevent its consequences. This may result in better results for people and families as well as lessen the general negative effects of trauma on society.

Two

TRAUMA-INFORMED PRACTICES IN COUNSELLING AND THERAPY

A set of guidelines known as trauma-informed practices can be used in therapy and counseling to provide a secure and comforting atmosphere for patients who have suffered trauma. These approaches are predicated on the knowledge that trauma can have a significant influence on an individual's physical, emotional, and psychological health and that individuals who have undergone trauma may not benefit from standard counseling and treatment methods.

Trauma-informed counseling and therapy is based on the following principles:

Safety: Making sure the client's physical and mental well-being come first.

Trustworthiness and transparency: Developing a

relationship of trust with the client by being truthful, forthright, and consistent in both actions and communications.

Collaboration and mutuality: Working in tandem with the client to create a customized treatment plan and attend to their needs; promoting peer support and mutual self-help among clients who have experienced trauma.

Empowerment, voice, and choice: Offering the client a say in their own rehabilitation and enabling them to make educated decisions about their course of treatment.

Cultural, historical, and gender issues: Acknowledging and honoring the distinctions in culture, history, and gender that may affect how trauma affects clients and how they react to it.

The following are some particular instances of trauma-informed counseling and therapeutic techniques:

Establishing a private, welcoming, and safe space for counseling sessions; this includes clearing the space of any potential triggers or reminders of trauma.

Using language that is non-blaming and empowering; this entails refraining from using language that places blame on the client for their trauma and putting the client's strengths and resilience front and center

Trauma education for the client: This aids in the client's comprehension of their symptoms and the impact of their trauma.

Teaching coping skills: This helps the client learn healthy coping mechanisms for managing their symptoms and stress.

Providing psychoeducation about trauma-related disorders: This helps the client understand the various types of trauma-related disorders, as well as the symptoms and treatment options for each.

Providing support for recovery:This includes assisting the client in connecting with support groups and other resources, as well as advocating for them in their community.

Advantages of Trauma-Informed Counseling and Therapy Techniques

An increasing amount of scholarly literature bolsters the application of trauma-informed approaches in therapy and counseling. The following are a few advantages of these practices:

Enhanced client engagement: Patients who feel safe and supported in therapy are more likely to attend sessions and actively engage in their treatment.

Improved client outcomes: Patients who receive trauma-informed care are more likely to see a decrease in symptoms and an improvement in their general quality of life.

Decreased risk of re-traumatization: Clients may not experience re-traumatization during the therapy process if trauma-informed approaches are used.

Enhanced therapist well-being: Trauma-informed therapists are less likely to burn out or suffer from recurrent trauma.

Using trauma-informed techniques is crucial to giving clients who have suffered trauma successful counseling and treatment. Therapists can assist clients heal from their experiences and create a safe and supportive environment by implementing these techniques.

TRAUMA-INFORMED APPROACHES IN EDUCATION

A collection of guidelines and procedures known as trauma-informed approaches to education can be applied to establish a secure and encouraging learning environment for students who have suffered trauma. These methods are predicated on the knowledge that a student's capacity to learn and behave can be significantly impacted by trauma, and that students who have experienced trauma may not benefit from conventional teaching methods.

Trauma-informed education is based on the following principles:

Safety: Making sure that every student's physical and mental well-being is given first priority.

Trustworthiness and transparency: Establishing trust with kids and families by open, sincere, and consistent communication and behavior.

Encouraging students who have experienced trauma to support one another and take care of themselves.

Collaboration and mutuality: Working together with students, families, and other stakeholders to create a personalized learning plan and meet each student's needs.

Recognizing and respecting the cultural, historical, and

gender-based differences that may influence how students experience and respond to trauma.

Empowerment, voice, and choice: Giving students a voice in their own learning and empowering them to make informed decisions about their education.

The following are particular instances of trauma-informed teaching strategies:

Creating a safe and inviting school climate entails establishing ground rules for behavior, giving students the chance to form wholesome bonds with peers and adults, and putting safety and wellbeing policies into place throughout the entire school.

The implementation of positive behavior interventions and supports, or PBIS, is a strategy that aims to prevent problem behaviors and foster positive social and emotional development in schools.

Offering social and emotional learning (SEL): SEL is a collection of abilities that support students in developing relationships, controlling their emotions, and making moral decisions.

Trauma training for educators and staff: Teachers and staff can benefit from trauma training by learning how trauma affects students' behavior and learning, as well as by creating useful plans for assisting traumatized students.

Working together with families: Families are an important source of support for students who have suffered trauma. Schools that are aware of trauma should endeavor to establish trusting bonds with families and include them in the educational and therapeutic processes for their students.

Advantages of Trauma-Informed Methods in Teaching

An increasing number of studies back up the application of trauma-informed teaching strategies. The following are a few advantages of these strategies:

Enhanced student outcomes: Students who attend trauma-informed schools are more likely to see improvements in their conduct, academic performance, and attendance in addition to a decrease in symptoms.

Decreased risk of re-traumatization: Trauma-informed practices can help to prevent students from experiencing trauma again.

Students who feel safe and supported in school are more likely to participate actively in their learning.

Improved teacher well-being: Burnout and vicarious trauma are less common among educators who employ trauma-informed techniques.

Using trauma-informed teaching strategies is crucial to giving every student a successful education. By implementing these strategies, educators can help every student realize their potential and establish a secure and encouraging learning environment.

TRAUMA-INFORMED PRACTICES IN HEALTHCARE SETTINGS

A set of guidelines and procedures known as trauma-informed practices (TIC) can be applied to provide patients who have suffered trauma with a secure and encouraging environment. These procedures are founded on the knowledge that patients who have suffered trauma may not respond well to conventional medical procedures and that trauma can have a significant and long-lasting influence on a patient's physical, emotional, and psychological health.

Trauma-informed healthcare encompasses the following principles:

Trustworthiness and transparency: Establishing trust with patients and staff by being truthful, forthright, and consistent in communication and behavior.

Safety: Ensuring that the physical and mental well-being of patients and personnel is of utmost importance.
Encouraging patients and staff who have experienced trauma to support one another and themselves.

Collaboration and mutuality: Working together with patients, families, and other stakeholders to create a customized treatment plan and attend to each patient's needs.

Cultural, historical, and gender issues: Acknowledging and respecting the cultural, historical, and gender-based differences that may influence how patients experience and respond to trauma.

Empowerment, voice, and choice: Giving patients a voice in their own care and empowering them to make informed decisions about their healthcare.

The following are particular instances of trauma-informed procedures that can be applied in medical environments:

Establishing a private, comfortable space for patient care ; this involves clearing out any potential triggers or reminders of trauma.

Using language that is non-blaming and empowering; this entails refraining from using language that places blame on the patient for their trauma and instead emphasizing their strengths and resilience.

Experience Education: This aids the patient in comprehending their symptoms and the impact of their experience.

Teaching coping skills: This helps the patient learn healthy coping mechanisms for managing their symptoms and stress. * **Providing psychoeducation about trauma-related disorders

This helps the patient understand the various types of trauma-related disorders, as well as the symptoms and treatment options for each.

Providing support for recovery: This includes assisting the patient in connecting with support groups and other resources, as well as advocating for them in their community.

Advantages of Trauma-Informed Care in Medical Environments

The application of trauma-informed techniques in healthcare settings is being bolstered by an increasing amount of research. The following are a few advantages of these practices:

Enhanced patient outcomes: Patients who receive trauma-informed care are more likely to see a decrease in symptoms and an improvement in their general quality of life.

Increased patient engagement: Patients are more likely to attend appointments and actively engage in their treatment when they feel safe and supported in their healthcare.

Reduced risk of re-traumatization: Trauma-informed practices can mitigate the risk of patients experiencing trauma again.

Enhanced well-being of providers: Healthcare professionals who employ trauma-informed methods are at a lower risk of burnout and recurrent trauma.

In order to effectively treat patients who have suffered trauma, trauma-informed treatments are a must. Healthcare professionals can assist patients heal from their experiences and provide a secure and supportive environment by implementing these techniques.

TRAUMA-INFORMED INTERVENTION IN CHILD WELFARE AND SOCIAL SERVICES

In child welfare and social services, trauma-informed interventions (TII) are a collection of ideas and methods that can be used to lessen the harmful consequences of trauma on kids and families. The foundation of TII is the knowledge that trauma is prevalent in the families that child welfare and social services assist, and that these families may not benefit from standard methods.

[Logo for social services and child welfare]

Trauma-informed intervention in child welfare and social services is based on the following principles:

Safety: Establishing a secure and nurturing atmosphere for kids, families, and employees.

Trustworthiness and transparency: Developing a relationship of trust with families by being truthful, forthright, and consistent in interactions and actions.

Collaboration and mutuality: Working together with families to create a customized plan to meet their needs.

Empowerment, voice, and choice: Providing parents with the tools they need to make decisions about their children's care and giving them a say in their own cases.

Cultural, historical, and gender issues: Acknowledging and honoring the unique cultural, historical, and gender-based distinctions among families.

The following are some particular instances of trauma-informed practices that social services and child welfare can implement:

Trauma screening: All families that get assistance from social services and child welfare ought to undergo trauma screening. Numerous tools, including questionnaires and interviews, can be used for this.

Offering trauma-informed training: All employees who interact with children and families ought to go through trauma-informed training. The effects of trauma on kids and families as well as how to give care that is trauma-informed should be included in this training.

Building a trauma-informed physical environment: Child welfare and social care organizations should provide a secure and encouraging physical space for kids and families. This entails providing a quiet, welcoming environment for meetings and getting rid of everything that can serve as a trigger or memory of past trauma.

Using empowering and non-criticizing language: Staff members should refrain from blaming parents for their children's distress. Rather, the emphasis needs to be on the resilience and qualities of parents.

Offering trauma psychoeducation: Parents who want to better understand their children's symptoms and the effects of trauma on them can benefit from psychoeducation.

Training coping skills: A range of coping techniques can be given to parents to assist them in controlling their own symptoms and handling stress.

Offering assistance for healing: As part of this, assist parents in making connections with various services and support groups.

Advantages of trauma-informed intervention in social services and child welfare:

The application of trauma-informed therapies in child welfare and social services is being bolstered by an increasing corpus of research. The following are a few advantages of these interventions:

Better outcomes for kids: Kids who get trauma-informed care are more likely to see a decrease in symptoms and an improvement in their general well-being.

Better family engagement: Parents who feel supported and safe are more likely to get involved in their kids' care.

Decreased risk of re-traumatization: Trauma-informed interventions can help keep kids and families from experiencing trauma from the child welfare system again.

Enhanced staff well-being: Staff members who employ trauma-informed practices are less likely to burn out and experience secondary trauma.

Effective child welfare and social care delivery requires trauma-informed approaches. Child welfare and social services organizations can assist children and families heal from their traumas by implementing these treatments and providing a safe and nurturing environment.

Three

CREATING ORGANISATIONAL CHANGE AND TRAUMA-INFORMED SYSTEMS

The process of implementing organizational transformation and trauma-informed systems is intricate and calls for leadership commitment, a thorough plan, and continuous assessment.

Dedication to Leadership

Getting the support of the leadership is the first step towards developing trauma-informed systems and organizational change. It follows that in order to build a more trauma-informed organization, leaders at all levels must be ready to make the required adjustments and have a thorough understanding of the effects that trauma has on people, families, and communities.

All-inclusive Scheme

The next stage once leadership commits is to create a detailed plan for trauma-informed systems and organizational change. This strategy should outline the precise definition of trauma-informed treatment as well as the organization's aims and objectives. The resources required to put the changes into practice should also be listed in the plan.

Continuous Assessment

Ultimately, it is critical to assess how well the modifications have worked. This will assist in determining the areas in which the company still needs to improve.

The following are particular tactics that can be employed to establish trauma-informed systems and organizational change:

Conduct a trauma assessment: To determine the incidence and consequences of trauma within the organization, a trauma assessment is the first step. There are several ways to carry out this assessment, including focus groups, interviews, and surveys.

Create a policy influenced by trauma: Following the completion of the trauma assessment, the company ought to create a trauma-informed policy. The organization's commitment to providing trauma-informed care should be outlined in this policy, along with particular protocols for trauma screening, assessment, and treatment.

Offer trauma-informed training: Trauma-informed

training ought to be given to all employees. The effects of trauma on people, families, and communities, as well as how to offer care that is trauma-informed, should be included in this training.

Establish a trauma-informed physical space: For those who have suffered trauma, the organization's physical space should be secure and encouraging. This entails providing a quiet, welcoming environment for meetings and getting rid of everything that can serve as a trigger or memory of past trauma.

Use language that is empowering and non-blaming: Employees should refrain from speaking in a way that places blame for trauma on specific people. Rather, the emphasis needs to be on the resilience and strengths of each individual.

Offer assistance in recuperation: The group ought to offer assistance to people who have suffered from trauma. As part of this, assist them in making connections with various services and support groups.

Difficulties in Developing Trauma-Informed Systems and Organizational Change

The development of trauma-informed systems and organizational change is fraught with difficulties. Among the most typical difficulties are:

Resistance to change: Employees may be reluctant to implement new procedures, particularly if they are unaware of the effects of trauma.

Resource shortage: It's possible that organizations lack the funding needed to adopt trauma-informed procedures.

Lack of leadership support: Organizational change can be challenging to implement without the backing of the leadership.

An increasing amount of evidence backs the use of trauma-informed strategies in companies, despite these obstacles. There are several advantages for organizations that successfully implement trauma-informed systems and organizational change, including:

Enhanced worker morale and productivity: Trauma-informed procedures can contribute to the development of a more encouraging and empowered workplace, which can enhance worker morale and productivity.

Decreased risk of lawsuits: Companies that implement

trauma-informed practices may be less vulnerable to lawsuits alleging discrimination or negligence.

Improved reputation: Companies that are well-known for providing trauma-informed care may enhance their standing in the community.

Although it's a difficult process, developing trauma-informed systems and organizational change is crucial. Through the adoption of trauma-informed practices, organizations can foster a more secure and encouraging atmosphere for all parties concerned.

TRAUMA-INFORMED COMMUNITY DEVELOPMENT

The goal of trauma-informed community development (TICD) is to create and support communities that are resilient, healing, and healthy so that individuals are well enough to take advantage of opportunities and reach their full potential. This method of community development acknowledges the pervasiveness of trauma and its effects on people as individuals, families, and communities. The mission of TICD is to establish a community that is safe, encouraging, and empowering for all people—including those who have suffered trauma.

Trauma-Informed Community Development Principles

The knowledge that trauma can have a significant and long-lasting effect on people's lives is the foundation of TICD's tenets. Among these guidelines are:

Safety: Making sure that everyone in the community is physically and mentally safe is of utmost importance.

Trustworthiness and transparency: Establishing trust with community members by open, truthful, and consistent communication and behavior. Encouraging community members who have experienced trauma to support one another and help themselves.

Collaboration and mutuality: Working together with members of the community, organizations, and systems to create a customized plan to meet the needs of the community.

Recognizing and respecting the cultural, historical, and gender-based differences that may influence how community members experience and respond to trauma.

Empowerment, voice, and choice: Giving community members a voice in their own recovery and empowering them to make informed decisions about their community.

Trauma-Informed Community Development Strategies

The implementation of TICD can be done in a variety of ways. Three general categories can be used to group these strategies:

Avoidance tactics: The goal of these tactics is to stop trauma from happening in the first place. This could entail encouraging good parenting techniques, offering early childhood education, and lowering rates of violence in the neighborhood.

Strategies for intervention: These tactics are meant to help and heal those who have suffered from trauma. This could entail offering treatment for substance misuse, mental health services, and counseling guided by trauma.

Recuperation tactics: The goal of these tactics is to aid in the healing of traumatized communities. This could entail developing secure and encouraging housing, offering chances for employment, and fostering community resilience.

Advantages of Community Development Based on Trauma

The application of TICD has several advantages. Among these advantages are:

Enhanced community well-being: TICD can contribute to a decrease in drug addiction, violence, and criminal activity.

Increased economic opportunity: TICD can foster an atmosphere that is more encouraging for companies and entrepreneurs.

Reduced healthcare costs: TICD may result in fewer expensive medical services being used.

Improved quality of life: TICD may result in a happier and more contented existence for all community members.

The lives of individuals, families, and communities can be greatly impacted by the community development strategy known as TICD. Communities can make everyone's environment safer, healthier, and more profitable by putting TICD into practice.

Four

TRAUMA-INFORMED INTERVENTION WITH CHILDREN AND ADOLESCENTS

Young people who have suffered trauma can be supported and healed through the specialist practice of trauma-informed intervention (TII) when working with children and adolescents. It acknowledges the substantial and long-lasting effects trauma can have on a child's growth, feelings, actions, and general wellbeing.

Fundamentals of Trauma-Informed Care for Kids and Teenagers

Safety, trust, and empowerment are the three main tenets that underpin TII with kids and teenagers. Among these guidelines are:

Security: It is critical to protect children and teenagers both physically and emotionally. This entails establishing a secure and encouraging atmosphere, eliminating possible triggers, and showing compassion and understanding when a person exhibits symptoms of distress.

Transparency and Trustworthiness: Effective interaction with children and adolescents requires developing trust. This entails maintaining the child's confidentiality while communicating and acting in a way that is truthful, transparent, and consistent.

Partnership and reciprocity: Working together to create a customized plan that takes into account each child's and adolescent's particular needs and strengths is essential. This entails collaborating with them to accomplish common objectives and including them in decision-making.

A voice, choice, and empowerment: Giving kids and teenagers a say in their own recovery process and enabling them to make educated decisions about their care is crucial. This entails giving them knowledge that is age-appropriate, supporting their right to self-expression, and honoring their independence.

Cultural, Historical, and Gender Sensitivity: It's critical to acknowledge and honor the cultural, historical, and gender-based variations that may affect how trauma affects children and adolescents and how they process it. This entails comprehending the particular difficulties that various groups confront and adjusting treatments to suit certain cultural contexts.

Trauma-Informed Intervention Techniques for Kids and Teens

A variety of techniques are used in TII with kids and teenagers to cater to their unique requirements and developmental phases. These tactics could consist of:

Evaluation and Screening: For early intervention and assistance, it is essential to identify children and adolescents who have experienced trauma through screening methods and thorough assessments.

Traumatic Focused Therapy and Psychoeducation: In addition to trauma-focused therapeutic techniques, psychoeducation about trauma and its aftermath can aid in children's and teenagers' understanding of their experiences, the development of coping mechanisms, and the processing of their feelings.

Skill Enhancement and Beneficial Growth: Building resilience and creating a sense of well-being in children and adolescents requires teaching them good coping mechanisms, stress management strategies, and positive social-emotional development.

Involvement and Support from Families: Involving families in the intervention process is essential for addressing family dynamics, creating a network of support, and fostering family system repair.

Interventions Based in the Community: Providing

assistance to kids and teenagers via community-based programs, like after-school events, mentorship programs, and peer support groups, can create a sense of community, establish social links, and highlight strong role models.

Advantages of Trauma-Informed Intervention for Young People

TII has several advantages when used with kids and teenagers, such as:

Decreased Symptoms and Enhanced Mental Well-Being: Improved mental health outcomes can result from trauma-informed interventions that help lessen the symptoms of trauma, such as anxiety, sadness, and post-traumatic stress disorder (PTSD).

Improved Resilience and Coping Skills: Youngsters and teenagers learn effective coping skills to control their emotions, handle stress, and become resilient in the face of adversity.

Enhanced Social Integration and Academic Achievement: Increased participation in school activities, enhanced academic performance, and enhanced peer relationships can all be attributed to trauma-informed therapies.

Promoted Healing and Well-Being: TII helps kids and teenagers feel safer, more confident, and more in control of their life, which helps them recover from trauma and feel better overall.

One of the most important strategies for addressing the pervasive effects of trauma on youth is trauma-informed intervention with children and adolescents. Through the application of evidence-based techniques and a trauma-sensitive lens, TII can assist children and adolescents in their healing, resilience building, and potential realization. Putting money into TII is putting money into our children's futures, our communities' futures, and our society's future.

TRAUMA-INFORMED INTERVENTION WITH ADULTS

Trauma-informed intervention (TII) with adults is a specialized approach to supporting and healing adults who have experienced trauma. It recognizes the profound and lasting impact that trauma can have on an individual's physical, emotional, psychological, and social well-being.

Principles of Trauma-Informed Intervention with Adults

TII with adults is guided by a set of principles that prioritize safety, trust, empowerment, and collaboration. These principles include:

Safety: Ensuring the physical and emotional safety of adults is paramount. This involves creating a safe and supportive environment, removing potential triggers, and responding to signs of distress with empathy and understanding.

Trustworthiness and Transparency: Building trust with adults is essential for effective intervention. This involves being honest, open, and consistent in communication and actions, and respecting the individual's confidentiality.

Collaboration and Mutuality: Collaborating with adults to develop a personalized plan that addresses their unique needs and strengths is crucial. This involves involving them in decision-making, working together to achieve shared goals, and respecting their autonomy.

Empowerment, Voice, and Choice: Empowering adults to make informed decisions about their care and giving them a voice in their own healing process is essential. This involves providing age-appropriate information, encouraging self-expression, and respecting their autonomy.

Cultural, Historical, and Gender Sensitivity: Recognizing and respecting the cultural, historical, and gender-based differences that may influence how adults experience and respond to trauma is vital. This involves tailoring interventions to specific cultural contexts and understanding the unique challenges faced by different populations.

Strategies for Trauma-Informed Intervention with Adults

TII with adults encompasses a range of strategies that address their specific needs and life circumstances. These strategies may include:

Screening and Assessment: Identifying adults who have experienced trauma through screening tools and comprehensive assessments is crucial for early intervention and support.

Psychoeducation and Trauma-Focused Therapy: Providing psychoeducation about trauma and its effects, along with trauma-focused therapy approaches, can help adults understand their experiences, develop coping skills, and process their emotions.

Skill Building and Positive Development: Teaching adults healthy coping skills, stress management techniques, and promoting positive social-emotional development is essential for building resilience and fostering a sense of well-being.

Addressing Substance Abuse and Mental Health Issues: Addressing co-occurring substance abuse or mental health concerns is crucial for comprehensive treatment and overall recovery.

Promoting Social Support and Connections: Encouraging adults to connect with support groups, peer networks, and community resources can provide a sense of belonging, social connections, and access to practical assistance.

Benefits of Trauma-Informed Intervention with Adults

TII with adults offers a range of benefits, including:

Reduced Symptoms and Improved Mental Health: Trauma-informed interventions can help reduce symptoms of trauma, such as anxiety, depression, and PTSD, leading to improved mental health outcomes.

Enhanced Coping Skills and Resilience: Adults develop healthy coping mechanisms to manage stress, regulate emotions, and build resilience in the face of challenges.

Improved Interpersonal Relationships:

Trauma-informed interventions can contribute to better communication, conflict resolution skills, and healthier relationships with family, friends, and partners.

Increased Productivity and Life Satisfaction: Adults experience reduced stress, improved self-esteem, and greater overall life satisfaction, leading to increased productivity and engagement in life activities.

Promoted Healing and Recovery: TII fosters a sense of safety, trust, and empowerment, enabling adults to heal from trauma, regain a sense of control over their lives, and achieve personal fulfillment.

Trauma-informed intervention with adults is a crucial approach to addressing the widespread impact of trauma on individuals and communities. By employing a trauma-sensitive lens and implementing evidence-based strategies, TII can help adults heal, develop resilience, and reclaim their lives. Investing in TII is an investment in the well-being of our communities, the strength of our workplaces, and the overall health of our society.

TRAUMA-INFORMED INTERVENTION WITH SURVIVORS OF COMPLEX TRAUMA

Trauma-informed intervention (TII) with survivors of complex trauma is a specialized approach to supporting and healing individuals who have experienced multiple traumatic events over an extended period, often during childhood. Complex trauma can have a profound and lasting impact on a person's physical, emotional, and psychological well-being.

Principles of Trauma-Informed Intervention with Survivors of Complex Trauma

TII with survivors of complex trauma is guided by a set of principles that emphasize safety, trust, collaboration, and empowerment. These principles include:

Safety: Ensuring the physical and emotional safety of survivors is paramount. This involves creating a safe and supportive environment, removing potential triggers, and responding to signs of distress with empathy and understanding.

Trustworthiness and Transparency: Building trust with survivors is essential for effective intervention. This involves being honest, open, and consistent in communication and actions, and respecting the survivor's confidentiality.

Collaboration and Mutuality: Collaborating with

survivors to develop a personalized plan that addresses their unique needs and strengths is crucial. This involves involving them in decision-making, working together to achieve shared goals, and respecting their autonomy.

Empowerment, Voice, and Choice: Empowering survivors to make informed decisions about their care and giving them a voice in their own healing process is essential. This involves providing age-appropriate information, encouraging self-expression, and respecting their autonomy.

Cultural, Historical, and Gender Sensitivity: Recognizing and respecting the cultural, historical, and gender-based differences that may influence how survivors experience and respond to complex trauma is vital. This involves tailoring interventions to specific cultural contexts and understanding the unique challenges faced by different populations.

Strategies for Trauma-Informed Intervention with Survivors of Complex Trauma

TII with survivors of complex trauma encompasses a range of strategies that address their specific needs and complex histories. These strategies may include:

Comprehensive Assessment: Conducting a thorough assessment to understand the survivor's trauma history, current symptoms, and overall functioning is crucial for developing an effective treatment plan.

Trauma-Focused Therapy and Psychoeducation: Providing trauma-focused therapy approaches, such as EMDR (Eye Movement Desensitization and Reprocessing) and cognitive behavioral therapy (CBT), can help survivors process their traumatic experiences, develop coping skills, and reduce symptoms.

Addressing Developmental and Interpersonal Issues: Addressing developmental delays, attachment difficulties, and social-emotional challenges is essential for promoting healthy growth and relationships.

Promoting Self-Care and Wellness: Encouraging survivors to engage in self-care practices, such as exercise, mindfulness, and relaxation techniques, can help manage stress, improve emotional regulation, and promote overall well-being.

Addressing Substance Abuse and Mental Health Issues: Addressing co-occurring substance abuse or mental health concerns is crucial for comprehensive treatment and recovery.

Strengthening Social Support and Connections: Encouraging survivors to connect with support groups, peer networks, and community resources can provide a sense of belonging, social connections, and access to practical assistance.

Benefits of Trauma-Informed Intervention with Survivors of Complex Trauma

TII with survivors of complex trauma offers a range of benefits, including:

Reduced Symptoms and Improved Mental Health: Trauma-informed interventions can help reduce symptoms of trauma, such as anxiety, depression, PTSD, and dissociative disorders, leading to improved mental health outcomes.

Enhanced Coping Skills and Resilience: Survivors develop healthy coping mechanisms to manage stress, regulate emotions, and build resilience in the face of challenges.

Improved Self-Esteem and Self-Efficacy: Survivors experience increased self-worth, a sense of control over their lives, and greater confidence in their ability to cope with life's challenges.

Improved Interpersonal Relationships: Trauma-informed interventions can contribute to better communication, conflict resolution skills, and healthier relationships with family, friends, and partners.

Promoted Healing and Recovery: TII fosters a sense of safety, trust, and empowerment, enabling survivors to heal from complex trauma, reclaim their lives, and achieve personal fulfillment.

Trauma-informed intervention with survivors of complex trauma is a critical approach to addressing the widespread and profound impact of complex trauma on individuals and communities. By employing a trauma-sensitive lens and implementing evidence-based strategies, TII can help survivors heal, develop resilience, and reclaim their lives. Investing in TII is an investment in the well-being of our communities, the strength of our relationships, and the overall resilience of our society.

THE FUTURE OF TRAUMA INFORMED CARE

Trauma-informed care (TIC) is a set of principles and practices that can help prevent and address the negative effects of trauma on individuals, families, and communities. TIC is based on the understanding that trauma is common and that traditional healthcare practices may not be effective for people who have experienced trauma.

The future of trauma-informed care is bright. There is a growing body of research that supports the use of TIC, and more and more healthcare providers and organizations are adopting TIC practices. Additionally, there is a growing awareness of the importance of TIC in other settings, such as schools, workplaces, and the criminal justice system.

Here are some of the key trends that are shaping the future of trauma-informed care:

A growing focus on prevention:*There is a growing recognition that the best way to address trauma is to prevent it from happening in the first place. This includes providing early childhood education, promoting positive parenting practices, and reducing community violence.

A more holistic approach to care: TIC is increasingly being seen as a holistic approach to care that addresses the physical, emotional, and social needs of people who have experienced trauma. This includes providing trauma-focused therapy, as well as support for housing, employment, and education.

A greater emphasis on cultural competency: TIC is increasingly being tailored to the specific needs of different cultural groups. This includes understanding the different ways that people from different cultures experience and respond to trauma.

The use of technology: Technology is being used to develop new and innovative ways to provide TIC. This includes using virtual reality to help people with PTSD, and using mobile apps to provide support and resources for people who have experienced trauma.

The future of trauma-informed care is full of promise. By adopting TIC practices, we can help to create a world where everyone has the opportunity to heal from trauma and live a healthy and fulfilling life.

www.ingramcontent.com/pod-product-compliance
Lightning Source LLC
Chambersburg PA
CBHW070805260726
48660CB00005B/1717
9798867447748